GEORGE BUCHANAN : GEORGE BUCHANAN WAS A SCOTTISH HISTORIAN AND HUMANIST SCHOLAR.

GOLU KUMAR

Copyright © Golu Kumar
All Rights Reserved.

This book has been published with all efforts taken to make the material error-free after the consent of the author. However, the author and the publisher do not assume and hereby disclaim any liability to any party for any loss, damage, or disruption caused by errors or omissions, whether such errors or omissions result from negligence, accident, or any other cause.

While every effort has been made to avoid any mistake or omission, this publication is being sold on the condition and understanding that neither the author nor the publishers or printers would be liable in any manner to any person by reason of any mistake or omission in this publication or for any action taken or omitted to be taken or advice rendered or accepted on the basis of this work. For any defect in printing or binding the publishers will be liable only to replace the defective copy by another copy of this work then available.

Contents

I

The scholar, in the sixteenth century, was a far more important personage than now. The supply of learned men was very small, the demand for the very great. During the whole of the fifteenth, and a great part of the sixteenth century, the human mind turned more and more from the scholastic philosophy of the Middle Ages to that of the Romans and the Greeks; and found more and more in old Pagan Art an element which Monastic Art had not, and which was yet necessary for the satisfaction of their craving after the Beautiful. At such a crisis of thought and taste, it was natural that the classical scholar, the man who knew old Rome, and still more old Greece, should usurp the place of the monk, a teacher of mankind; and that scholars should form, for a while, a new and powerful aristocracy, limited and privileged, and all the more redoubtable, because its power lay in intellect, and had been won by intellect alone.

Those who, whether poor or rich, did not fear the monk and priest, at least feared the "scholar," who held, so the vulgar believed, the keys of that magic lore by which the old necromancers had built cities like Rome, and worked marvels of mechanical and chemical skill, which the degenerate modern could never equal.

If the "scholar" stopped in a town, his hostess probably begged of him a charm against toothache or rheumatism. The penniless knight discoursed his alchemy and the chances of retrieving his fortune by the art of transmuting metals into gold. The queen or bishop worried him in private about casting their nativities and finding their fates among the stars. But the statesman, who dealt with more practical matters, hired him as an advocate and rhetorician, who could fight his master's enemies with the weapons of Demosthenes and Cicero. Wherever the scholar's steps were turned, he might be master of others, as long as he was master of himself. The complaints which he so often uttered concerning the cruelty of fortune, the fickleness of princes, and so forth, were probably no more just then than such complaints are now. Then, as now, he got his deserts; and the world bought him at his price. If he chose to sell himself to this patron and to that, he was used and thrown away: if he chose to remain in honorable independence, he was courted and feared.

Among the successful scholars of the sixteenth century, none surely is more notable than George Buchanan. The poor Scotch widow's son, by force of native wit, and, as I think, by force of native worth, fights his way upward, through poverty and severest persecution, to become the correspondent and friend of the greatest literary celebrities of the Continent, comparable, in their opinion, to the best Latin poets of antiquity; the preceptor of princes; the counselor and spokesman of Scotch statesmen in the most dangerous of times; and leaves behind him political treatises, which have influenced not only the history of his own country, but that of the civilized world.

Such a success could not be attained without making enemies, perhaps without making mistakes. But the more we study George Buchanan's history, the less we shall be inclined to hunt out his failings, the more inclined to admire his worth. A shrewd, sound-hearted, affectionate man, with a strong love of right and scorn of wrong, and humor withal which saved him--except on really great occasions--from bitterness, and helped him to laugh where narrower natures would have only snarled,--he is, in many respects, a type of those Lowland Scots, who long preserved his jokes, genuine or reputed, as a common household book. {1 A schoolmaster by profession, and struggling for long years amid the temptations which, in those days, degraded his class into cruel and sordid pedants, he rose from the mere pedagogue to be, in the best sense of the word, a courtier: "One," says Daniel Heinsius, "who seemed not only born for a court but born to amend it. He brought to his queen that at which she could not wonder enough. For, by affecting certain liberty in censuring morals, he avoided all offense, under the cloak of simplicity." Of him and his compeers, Turnebus, and Mauritius, and their friend Andrea Govea, Ronsard, the French court poet, said that they had nothing of the pedagogue about them but the gown and cap. "Austere in the face, and rustic in his looks," says David Buchanan, "but most polished in style and speech; and continually, even in serious conversation, jesting most wittily." "Rough-hewn, slovenly, and rude," says Peacham, in his "Compleat Gentleman," speaking of him, probably, as he appeared old, "in his person, behavior, and fashion; seldom caring for a better outside than a rugged-gown girt close about him: yet his inside and concept in poesie was most rich, and his sweetness and facilities in verse most excellent." A typical Lowland Scot, as I said just now, he seems to have absorbed all the best culture that France could afford him, without losing the strength, honesty, and humor that he inherited from his Stirlingshire kindred. Such a success could not be attained without making enemies, perhaps without making mistakes. But the more we study George Buchanan's history, the less we shall be inclined to hunt out his failings, the more inclined to admire his worth. A shrewd, sound-hearted, affectionate man, with a strong love of right and scorn of wrong, and humor withal which saved him--except on really great occasions--from bitterness, and helped him to laugh where narrower natures would have only snarled,--he is, in many respects, a type of those Lowland Scots, who long preserved his jokes, genuine or reputed, as a common household book. {16} A schoolmaster by profession, and struggling for long years amid the temptations which, in those days, degraded his class into cruel and sordid pedants, he rose from the mere pedagogue to be, in the best sense of the word, a courtier: "One," says Daniel Heinsius, "who seemed not only born for a court but born to amend it. He brought to his queen that at which she could not wonder enough. For, by affecting certain liberty in censuring morals, he avoided all offense, under the cloak of simplicity." Of him and his compeers, Turnebus, and Mauritius, and their friend Andrea Govea, Ronsard, the French court poet, said that they had nothing of the pedagogue about them but the gown and cap. "Austere in the face, and rustic in his looks," says David Buchanan, "but most polished in style and speech; and continually, even in serious conversation, jesting most wittily." "Rough-hewn, slovenly, and rude," says Peacham, in his "Compleat Gentleman," speaking of him, probably, as he appeared old, "in his person, behavior, and fashion; seldom caring for a better outside than a rugged-gown girt close about him: yet his inside and concept in poesie was most rich, and his sweetness and facilities in verse most excellent." A typical Lowland Scot, as I said just now, he seems to have absorbed all the best culture that France could afford him, without losing the strength, honesty, and humor that he inherited from his Stirlingshire kindred.

The story of his life is easily traced. When an old man, he wrote down the main events of it, at the request of his friends; and his sketch has been filled out by commentators, if not always favorable, at least erudite. Born in 1506, at the Moss, in Killearn--where an obelisk to his memory, so one reads, has been erected in this century--of a family "rather ancient than rich," his father died in the prime of manhood, his grandfather a spendthrift, he and his seven brothers and sisters were brought up by a widowed mother, Agnes Heriot--of whom one wishes to know more; for the rule that great sons have great mothers probably holds good in her case. George gave signs, while at the village school, of future scholarship; and when he was only fourteen, his uncle James sent him to the University of Paris. Those were hard times; and the youths, or rather boys, who meant to become scholars, had a cruel life of it, cast desperately out on the wide world to beg and starve, either into self-restraint and success or into the ruin of body and soul. And a cruel life George had. Within two years he was down in a severe illness, his uncle died, his supplies stopped, and the boy of sixteen got home, he does not tell how. Then he tried soldiering; and was with Albany's French Auxiliaries at the ineffectual attack on Wark Castle. Marching back through deep snow, he got a fresh illness, which kept him in bed all winter. Then he and his brother were sent to St. Andrews, where he got his B.A. at nineteen. The next summer he went

to France once more; and "fell," he says, "into the flames
of the Lutheran sect, which was then spreading far and
wide." Two years of penury followed; and then three years
of school-mastering in the College of St. Barbe, which he has
immortalized--at least, for the few who care to read modern
Latin poetry--in his elegy on "The Miseries of a Parisian
Teacher of the Humanities." The wretched regent-master,
pale and suffering, sits up all night preparing his lecture,
biting his nails and thumping his desk; and falls asleep for
a few minutes, to start up at the sound of the four-o'clock
bell, and be in school by five, his Virgil in one hand, and his
rod in the other, trying to do work on his account at old
manuscripts and bawling all the while at his wretched boys,
who cheat him and pay each other to answer to truants'
names. The class is all wrong. "One is barefoot, another's
shoe is burst, another cries, another writes home. Then
comes the rod, the sound of blows, and howls; and the day
passes in tears." "Then mass, then another lesson, then more
blows; there is hardly time to eat." I have no space to finish
the picture of the stupid misery which, Buchanan says, was
ruining his intellect, while it starved his body. However,
happier days came. Gilbert Kennedy, Earl of Cassilis, who
seems to have been a noble young gentleman, took him as
his tutor for the next five years; and with him, he went back
to Scotland.

But there his plain speaking got him, as it did more than
once afterward, into trouble. He took it into his head to
write, in imitation of Dunbar, a Latin poem, in which St.
Francis asks him in a dream to become a Gray Friar, and
Buchanan answered in language which had the unpleasant
fault of being too clever, and--to judge from contemporary
evidence--only too true. The friars said nothing at first; but
when King James made Buchanan tutor to one of his

natural sons, they, "men professing meekness, took the matter somewhat more angrily than befitted men so pious in the opinion of the people." So Buchanan himself puts it: but, to do the poor friars justice, they must have been angels, not men, if they did not writhe somewhat under the scourge which he had laid on them. To be told that there was hardly a place in heaven for monks was hard to hear and bear. They accused him to the king of heresy; but not being then in favor with James, they got no answer, and Buchanan was commanded to repeat the castigation. Having found out that the friars were not to be touched with impunity, he wrote, he says, a short and ambiguous poem. But the king, who loved a joke, demanded something sharp and stinging, and Buchanan obeyed by writing, but not publishing, "The Franciscans," a long satire, compared to which the "Somnium" was bland and merciful. The storm rose. Cardinal Beaten, Buchanan says, wanted to buy him of the king, and then, of course, burn him, as he had just burnt five poor souls; so, knowing James's avarice, he fled to England, through freebooters and pestilence.

There he found, he says, "men of both factions being burned on the same day and in the same fire"--a pardonable exaggeration--"by Henry VIII., in his old age more intent on his safety than on the purity of religion." So to his beloved France, he went again, to find his enemy Beaten ambassador in Paris. The capital was too hot to hold him; and he fled south to Bordeaux, to Andrea Govea, the Portuguese principal of the College of Guienne. As Professor of Latin at Bordeaux, we find him presenting a Latin poem to Charles V.; and indulging that fancy of his for Latin poetry which seems to us nowadays a childish pedantry, which was then--when Latin was the vernacular tongue of all scholars--a serious, if not altogether a useful, pursuit.

Of his tragedies, so famous in their day--the "Baptist," the "Medea," the "Jephtha," and the "Alcestis"--there is neither space nor need to speak here, save to notice the bold declarations in the "Baptist" against tyranny and priestcraft; and to notice also that these tragedies gained for the poor Scotsman, in the eyes of the best scholars of Europe, a credit amounting almost to veneration. When he returned to Paris, he found occupation at once; and, as his Scots biographers love to record, "three of the most learned men in the world taught humanity in the same college," viz. Turnebus, Mauritius, and Buchanan.

Then followed a strange episode in his life. A university had been founded at Coimbra, in Portugal, and Andrea Govea had been invited to bring thither what French savants he could collect. Buchanan went to Portugal with his brother Patrick, two more Scotsmen, Dempster and Ramsay, and a goodly company of French scholars, whose names and histories may be read in the erudite pages of Dr. Irving, went likewise. All prospered in the new Temple of the Muses for a year or so. Then its high-priest, Govea, died; and, by a peripeteia too common in those days and countries, Buchanan and two of his friends migrated unwillingly from the Temple of the Muses for that of Moloch, and found themselves in the Inquisition.

Buchanan, it seems, had said that St. Augustine was more of a Lutheran than a Catholic on the question of the mass. He and his friends had eaten flesh in Lent; which, he says, almost everyone in Spain did. But he was suspected, and with reason, as a heretic; the Gray Friars formed but one brotherhood throughout Europe, and news among them traveled surely if not fast so that the story of the satire written in Scotland had reached Portugal. The culprits were imprisoned, examined, and bullied--but not tortured--for a year and a half. At the end of that time, the proofs of heresy, it seems, were insufficient; but lest says Buchanan with honest pride, "they should get the reputation of having vainly tormented a man not altogether unknown," they sent him for some months to a monastery, to be instructed by the monks. "The men," he says, "were neither inhuman nor bad, but utterly ignorant of religion;" and Buchanan solaced himself during the intervals of their instructions, by beginning his Latin translation of the Psalms.

At last, he got free and begged leave to return to France, but in vain. And so, wearied out, he got on board a Candian ship at Lisbon and escaped to England. But England, he says, during the anarchy of Edward VI.'s reign, was not land that suited him; and he returned to France, to fulfill the hopes which he had expressed in his charming "Desiderium Lutitiae," and the still more charming, because more simple, "Adventus in Gilliam," in which he bids farewell, in most melodious verse, to "the hungry moors of wretched Portugal, and her clods fertile in naught but penury."

Some seven years succeeded of schoolmastering and verse-writing: the Latin paraphrase of the Psalms; another of the "Alcestis" of Euripides; an Epithalamium on the marriage of poor Mary Stuart, noble and sincere, however fantastic and pedantic, after the manner of the times; "Pomps," too, for her wedding, and for other public ceremonies, in which all the heathen gods and goddesses figure; epigrams, panegyrics, satires, much of which later productions he would have consigned to the dust-heap in his old age, had not his too fond friends persuaded him to republish the follies and coarsenesses of his youth. He was now one of the most famous scholars in Europe and the intimate friend of all the great literary men. Was he to go on to the end, die, and no more? Was he to sink into the mere pedant; or, if he could not do that, into the mere court versifier?

The wars of religion saved him, as they saved many other noble souls, from that degradation. The events of 1560-62 forced Buchanan, as they forced many a learned man besides, to choose whether he would be a child of light or a child of darkness; whether he would be a dilettante classicist or a preacher--it might be a martyr--of the Gospel. Buchanan may have left France in "The Troubles" merely to enjoy in his own country elegant and learned repose. He may have fancied that he had found it, when he saw himself, despite his public profession of adherence to the Reformed Kirk, reading Livy every afternoon with his exquisite young sovereign; master, by her favor, of the temporalities of Crossraguel Abbey, and by the favor of Murray, Principal of St. Leonard's College in St. Andrew's. Perhaps he fancied at times that "tomorrow was to be as today, and much more abundant;" that thenceforth he might read his folio, and write his epigram, and joke his joke, as a lazy comfortable pluralist, taking his morning stroll out to the corner where poor Wishart had been burned, above the blue sea and the yellow sands, and looking up to the castle tower from whence his enemy Beaton's corpse had been hung out; with the comfortable reflection that quieter times had come, and that whatever evil deeds Archbishop Hamilton might dare, he would not dare to put the Principal of St. Leonard's into the "bottle dungeon."

If such hopes ever crossed Geordie's keen fancy, they were disappointed suddenly and fearfully. The fire which had been kindled in France was to reach Scotland likewise. "Revolutions are not made with rose-water;" and the time was at hand when all good spirits in Scotland, and George

Buchanan among them, had to choose, once and for all, amid danger, confusion, terror, whether they would serve God or Mammon; for to serve both would be soon impossible.

Which side, in that war of light and darkness, George Buchanan took, is notorious. He saw then, as others have seen since, that the two men in Scotland who were capable of being her captains in the strife were Knox and Murray; and to them, he gave in his allegiance heart and soul.

This is the critical epoch in Buchanan's life. By his conduct to Queen Mary, he must stand or fall. I believe that he will stand. It is not my intention to enter into the details of a matter so painful, so shocking, so prodigious; and now that that question is finally set at rest, by the writings both of Mr. Froude and Mr. Burton, there is no need to allude to it further, save where Buchanan's name is concerned. One may now have every sympathy with Mary Stuart; one may regard with awe a figure so stately, so tragic, in one sense so heroic,--for she reminds one rather of the heroine of an old Greek tragedy, swept to her doom by some irresistible fate, than of a being of our flesh and blood, and of our modern and Christian times. One may sympathize with the great womanhood which charmed so many while she was alive; which has charmed, in later years, so many noble spirits who have believed in her innocence, and have doubtless been elevated and purified by their devotion to one who seemed to them an ideal being. So far from regarding her as a hateful personage, one may feel oneself forbidden to hate a woman whom God may have loved, and may have pardoned, to judge from the punishment so swift, and yet so enduring, which He inflicted. At least, he must so believe who holds that punishment is a sign of mercy; that the most dreadful of all dooms is impunity. Nay, more, those "Casket" letters and sonnets may be a relief to the mind of one who believes in her guilt on other grounds; a relief when one finds in them a tenderness, a sweetness, a delicacy, magnificent self-sacrifice, however hideously misplaced, which shows what a womanly heart was there; a heart which, joined to that queenly brain, might have made her a blessing and glory to Scotland, had not the whole character been warped and ruinate from childhood, by education so abominable, that anyone who knows what words she must have heard, what scenes she must have beheld in France, from her youth up, will wonder that she sinned so little: not that she sinned so much. One may feel, in a word, that there is every excuse for those who have asserted Mary's innocence because their high-mindedness shrank from believing her guilty: but yet Buchanan, in his place and time, may have felt as deeply that he could do no otherwise than he did.

The charges against him, as all readers of Scotch literature know well, may be reduced to two heads. 1st. The letters and sonnets were forgeries. Maitland of Lethington may have forged the letters; Buchanan, according to some, the sonnets. Whoever forged them, Buchanan made use of them in his Detection, knowing them to be forged. 2nd. Whether Mary was innocent or not, Buchanan acted a base and ungrateful part in putting himself in the forefront amongst her accusers. He had been her tutor, her pensioner. She had heaped him with favors; and, after all, she was his queen, and a defenseless woman: and yet he returned her kindness, in the hour of her fall, by invectives fit only for a rancorous and reckless advocate, determined to force a verdict by the basest arts of oratory.

Now as to the Casket letters. I should have thought they bore in themselves the best evidence of being genuine. I can add nothing to the arguments of Mr. Froude and Mr. Burton, save this: that no one clever enough to be a forger would have put together documents so incoherent, and so incomplete. For the evidence of guilt which they contain is, after all, slight and indirect, and superfluous altogether; seeing that Mary's guilt was open and palpable, before the supposed discovery of the letters, to every person at home and abroad who had any knowledge of the facts. As for the alleged inconsistency of the letters with proven facts: the answer is, that whosoever wrote the letters would be more likely to know facts which were taking place around them than any critic could be one hundred or three hundred years afterward. But if these mistakes as to facts exist in them, they are only a fresh argument for their authenticity. Mary, writing in agony and confusion, might easily make a mistake: forgers would only take too good care to make none.

But the strongest evidence in favor of the letters and sonnets, despite the arguments of good Dr. Whittaker and other apologists for Mary, is to be found in their tone. A forger in those coarse days would have made Mary write in some Semiramis or Roxana vein, utterly alien to the tenderness, the delicacy, the pitiful confusion of mind, the conscious weakness, the imploring and most feminine trust which makes the letters, to those who--as I do--believe in them, more pathetic than any fictitious sorrows which poets could invent. More than one touch, indeed, of utter self-abasement, in the second letter, is so unexpected, so subtle, and yet so true to the heart of woman, that--as has been well said--if it was invented there must have existed in Scotland an earlier Shakespeare; who yet has died without leaving any other sign, for good or evil, of his dramatic genius.

As for the theory (totally unsupported) that Buchanan forged the poem usually called the "Sonnets;" it is paying old Geordie's genius, however versatile it may have been, too high a compliment to believe that he could have written both them and the Detection; while it is paying his shrewdness too low a compliment to believe that he could have put into them, out of mere carelessness or stupidity, the well-known line, which seems incompatible with the theory both of the letters and his Detection; and which has ere now been brought forward as a fresh proof of Mary's innocence.

And, as with the letters, so with the sonnets: their delicacy, their grace, their reticence, are so many arguments against their having been forged by any Scot of the sixteenth century, and least of all by one in whose character--whatever his other virtues may have been--delicacy was by no means the strongest point.

As for the complaint that Buchanan was ungrateful to Mary, it must be said: That even if she, and not Murray, had bestowed on him the temporalities of Crossraguel Abbey four years before, it was merely fair pay for services fairly rendered; and I am not aware that payment, or even favors, however gracious, bind any man's soul and conscience in questions of highest morality and highest public importance. And the importance of that question cannot be exaggerated. At a moment when Scotland seemed struggling in death-throes of anarchy, civil and religious, and was in danger of becoming prey either to England or to France, if there could not be formed out of the heart of her a people, steadfast, trusty, united, strong politically because strong in the fear of God and the desire of righteousness-- at such a moment as this, a crime had been committed, the like of which had not been heard in Europe since the tragedy of Joan of Naples. All Europe stood aghast. The honor of the Scottish nation was at stake. More than Mary or Bothwell were known to be implicated in the deed; and-- as Buchanan puts it in the opening of his "De Jure Regni"-- "The fault of some few was charged upon all, and the common hatred of a particular person did redound to the whole nation; so that even such as were remote from any suspicion were inflamed by the infamy of men's crimes."

To vindicate the national honor, and to punish the guilty, as well as to save themselves from utter anarchy, the great majority of the Scotch nation had taken measures against Mary which required explicit justification in the sight of Europe, as Buchanan frankly confesses in the opening of his "De Jure Regni." The chief authors of those measures had been summoned, perhaps unwisely and unjustly, to answer for their conduct to the Queen of England. Queen Elizabeth--a fact which was notorious enough then, though it has been forgotten till the last few years--was doing her utmost to shield Mary. Buchanan was deputed, it seems, to speak out for the people of Scotland, and certainly never people had an abler apologist. If he spoke fiercely, savagely, it must be remembered that he spoke of a fierce and savage matter; if he used--and it may be abused--all the arts of oratory, it must be remembered that he was fighting for the honor, and it may be for the national life, of his country, and striking--as men in such cases have a right to strike--as hard as he could. If he makes no secret of his indignation, and even contempt, it must be remembered that indignation and contempt may well have been real with him, while they were real with the soundest part of his countrymen; with that reforming middle class, comparatively untainted by French profligacy, comparatively undebauched by feudal subservience, which has been the leaven which has leavened the whole Scottish people in the last three centuries with the elements of their greatness. If finally, he heaps up against the unhappy Queen charges which Mr. Burton thinks incredible, it must be remembered that, as he well says, these changes give the popular feeling about Queen Mary; and it must be remembered also, that that popular feeling need not have been altogether unfounded. Incredible stories, thank God, in these milder days, were credible enough then, because, alas! they were so often true. Things more ugly than any related of poor Mary were possible enough--as no one knew better than Buchanan--in that very French court in which Mary had been brought up; things as ugly were possible in Scotland then, and for at least a century later; and while we may hope that Buchanan has overstated his case, we must not blame him too severely for yielding to a temptation common to all men of genius when their creative power is roused to its highest energy by a great cause and great indignation.

And that the genius was there, no man can doubt; one cannot read that "hideously eloquent" description of Kirk o' Field, which Mr. Burton has well chosen as a specimen of Buchanan's style, without seeing that we are face to face with a genius of a very lofty order: not, indeed, of the loftiest--for there is always in Buchanan's work, it seems to me, a want of unconsciousness, and a want of tenderness-- but still a genius worthy to be placed beside those ancient writers from whom he took his manner. Whether or not we agree with his contemporaries, who say that he equaled Virgil in Latin poetry, we may place him fairly as a prose writer by the side of Demosthenes, Cicero, or Tacitus. And so I pass from this painful subject; only quoting--if I may be permitted to quote--Mr. Burton's wise and gentle verdict on the whole. "Buchanan," he says, "though a zealous Protestant, had a good deal of the Catholic and skeptical spirit of Erasmus, and an admiring eye for everything great and beautiful. Like the rest of his countrymen, he bowed himself in presence of the luster that surrounded the early career of his mistress. More than once he expressed his pride and reverence in the inspiration of a genius deemed by his contemporaries to be worthy of the theme. There is not, perhaps, to be found elsewhere in literature so solemn a memorial of shipwrecked hopes, of a sunny opening and a stormy end, as one finds in turning the leaves of the volume which contains the beautiful epigram 'Nympha Caledoniae' in one part, the 'Detection Mariae Reginae' in another; and this contrast is, no doubt, a faithful parallel of the reaction in the popular mind. This reaction seems to have been general, and not limited to the Protestant party; for the conditions under which it became almost a part of the creed of the Church of Rome to believe in her innocence had not arisen."

If Buchanan, as some of his detractors have thought, raised himself by subserviency to the intrigues of the Regent Murray, the best heads in Scotland seem to have been of a different opinion. The murder of Murray did not involve Buchanan's fall. He had avenged it, as far as pen could do it, by that "Admonition Direct to the Trew Lordis," in which he showed himself as great a master of Scottish, as he was of Latin prose. His satire of the "Chameleon," though its publication was stopped by Maitland, must have been read in manuscript by many of those same "True Lords;" and though there were nobler instincts in Maitland than any Buchanan gave him credit for, the satire breathed honest indignation against that wily turncoat's misdoings, which could not but recommend the author to all honest men.

Therefore it was, I presume, and not because he was a rogue, and a hired literary spadassin, that to the best heads in Scotland he seemed so useful, it may be so worthy, a man, that he be provided with continually increasing employment. As tutor to James I.; as director, for a short time, of the chancery; as keeper of the privy seal, and privy councilor; as one of the commissioners for codifying the laws, and again--for in the semi-anarchic state of Scotland, the government had to do everything in the way of organization--in the committee for promulgating a standard Latin grammar; in the committee for reforming the University of St. Andrew's: in all these Buchanan's talents were, again and again, called for, and always ready. The value of his work, especially that for the reform of St. Andrew's, must be judged by Scotsmen, rather than by an Englishman; but all that one knows of it justifies Melville's sentence in the well-known passage in his memoirs, wherein he describes the tutors and household of the young king. "Mr. George was a Stoic philosopher, who looked not far before him;" in plain words, a high-minded and right-minded man bent on doing the duty which lay nearest him. The worst that can be said against him during these times is, that his name appears with the sum of 100 pounds against it, as one of those "who were to be entertained in Scotland by pensions out of England;" and Ruddiman, of course, comments on the fact by saying that Buchanan "was at length to act under the threefold character of malcontent, reformer, and pensioner:" but it gives no proof whatsoever that Buchanan ever received any such bribe; and in the very month, seemingly, in which that list was written--10th March 1579--Buchanan had given proof to the world that he was not likely to be bribed or bought, by publishing a book, as offensive probably to Queen Elizabeth as it was to his royal pupil; namely, his famous "De Jure Regni apud Scots," the very primer, according to many great thinkers, of constitutional liberty. He dedicates that book to King James, "not only as his monitor but also as an importunate and bold exactor, which in these his tender and flexible years may conduct him in safety past the rocks of flattery." He has complimented James already on his abhorrence of flattery, "his inclination far above his years for undertaking all heroical and noble attempts, his promptitude in obeying his instructors and governors, and all who give him sound admonition, and his judgment and diligence in examining affairs, so that no man's authority can have much weight with him unless it is confirmed by probable reasons." Buchanan may have thought that nine years of his stern rule had eradicated some of James's ill conditions; the petulance which made him kill the Master of Mar's sparrow, in trying to wrest it out of his hand; the carelessness with which--if the story told by Chytraeus, on the authority of Buchanan's nephew, be true--James signed away his crown to Buchanan for fifteen days, and only discovered his mistake by seeing Buchanan act in open court the character of King of Scots. Buchanan had, at last, made him a scholar; he may have fancied that he had made him likewise a manful man: yet he may have dreaded that, as James grew up, the old inclinations would return in stronger and uglier shapes, and that flattery might be, as it was, after all, the cause of James's moral ruin. He at least will be no flatterer. He opens the dialogue which he sends to the king, with a calm but distinct assertion of his mother's guilt, and a justification of the conduct of men who were now most of the past helping Buchanan, for they were laid in their graves; and then goes on to argue fairly, but to lay down firmly, in a sort of Socratic dialogue, those very principles by loyalty to which the House of Hanover has reigned, and will reign, over these realms. So with his History of Scotland; later antiquarian researches have destroyed the value of the earlier portions of it: but they have surely increased the value of those later portions, in which Buchanan inserted so much which he had already spoken out in his Detection of Mary. In that book also _liberavit animam suam_; he spoke his mind fearless of consequences, in the face of a king who he must have known--for Buchanan was no dullard--regarded him with deep dislike, who might in a few years be able to work his ruin.

But those few years were not given to Buchanan. He had all but done his work, and he hastened to get it over before the night should come wherein no man can work. One must be excused for telling--one would not tell it in a book intended to be read only by Scotsmen, who know or ought to know the tale already--how the two Melvilles and Buchanan's nephew Thomas went to see him in Edinburgh, in September 1581, hearing that he was ill, and his History still in the press; and how they found the old sage, true to his schoolmaster's instincts, teaching the Hornbook to his servant-lad; and how he told them that doing that was "better than stealing sheep, or sitting idle, which was as bad," and showed them that dedication to James I., in which he holds up to his imitation as a hero whose equal was hard to be found in history, that very King David whose liberality to the Romish Church provoked James's witticism that "David was a sair saint for the crown." Andrew Melville, so James Melville says, found fault with the style. Buchanan replied that he could do no more for thinking of another thing, which was to die. They then went to Arbuthnot's printing-house, and inspected the history, as far as that terrible passage concerning Rizzio's burial, where Mary is represented as "laying the miscreant almost in the arms of Maud de Valois, the late queen." Alarmed, and not without reason, at such plain speaking, they stopped the press and went back to Buchanan's house. Buchanan was in bed. "He was going," he said, "the way of welfare." They asked him to soften the passage; the king might prohibit the whole work. "Tell me, man," said Buchanan, "if I have told the truth." They could not, or would not, deny it. "Then I will abide his feud, and all his kin's; pray, pray to God for me, and let Him direct all." "So," says Melville, "before the printing of his chronicle was ended, this most learned, wise, and godly man ended his mortal life."

Camden has a hearsay story--written, it must be remembered, in James I.'s time--that Buchanan, on his death-bed, repented of his harsh words against Queen Mary; and an old Lady Rosyth is said to have said that when she was young a certain David Buchanan recollected hearing some such words from George Buchanan's mouth. Those who will, may read what Ruddiman and Love have said, and oversaid, on both sides of the question: whatever conclusion they come to, it will probably not be that to which George Chalmers comes in his life of Ruddiman: that "Buchanan, like other liars, who, by the repetition of falsehoods are induced to consider the fiction as truth, had so often dwelt with complacency on the forgeries of his Detections, and the figments of his History, that he at length regarded his fictions and his forgeries as most authentic facts."

At all events, his fictions and his forgeries had not paid him in that coin which base men generally consider the only coin worth having, namely, the good things of this life. He left nothing behind him--if at least Dr. Irving has rightly construed the "Testament Dative" which he gives in his appendix--save arrears to the sum of 100 pounds of his Crossraguel pension. We may believe as we choose the story in Mackenzie's "Scotch Writers" that when he felt himself dying, he asked his servant Young about the state of his funds, and finding he had not enough to bury himself withal, ordered what he had to be given to the poor, and said that if they did not choose to bury him they might let him lie where he was, or cast him in a ditch, the matter was very little to him. He was buried, it seems, at the expense of the city of Edinburgh, in the Greyfriars' Churchyard--one says in a plain turf grave--among the marble monuments which covered the bones of worse or meaner men; and whether or not the "Throughstone" which, "sunk under the ground in the Greyfriars," was raised and cleaned by the Council of Edinburgh in 1701, was really George Buchanan's, the reigning powers troubled themselves little for several generations where he lay.

For Buchanan's politics were too advanced for his age. Not only Catholic Scotsmen, like Blackwood, Winzer, and Ninian, but Protestants, like Sir Thomas Craig and Sir John Wemyss, could not stomach the "De Jure Regni." They may have had some reason on their side. In the then anarchic state of Scotland, organization and unity under a common head may have been more important than the assertion of popular rights. Be that as it may, in 1584, only two years after his death, the Scots Parliament condemned his Dialogue and History as untrue, and commanded all possessors of copies to deliver them up, that they might be purged of "the offensive and extraordinary matters" which they contained. The "De Jure Regni" was again prohibited in Scotland, in 1664, even in manuscript; and in 1683, the whole of Buchanan's political works had the honor of being burned by the University of Oxford, in company with those of Milton, Languet, and others, as "pernicious books, and damnable doctrines, destructive to the sacred persons of Princes, their state and government, and of all human society." And thus the seed which Buchanan had sown, and Milton had watered--for the allegation that Milton borrowed from Buchanan is probably true, and equally honorable to both--lay trampled into the earth, and seemingly lifeless, till it tillered out, and blossomed, and bore fruit to a good purpose, in the Revolution of 1688.

Tom Buchanan's clear head and stout heart, Scotland owes, as England owes likewise, much of her modern liberty. But Scotland's debt to him, it seems to me, is even greater on the count of morality, public and private. What the morality of the Scotch upper classes was like, in Buchanan's early days, is too notorious; and there remains proof enough--in the writings, for instance, of Sir David Lindsay--that the morality of the populace, which looked up to the nobles as its example and its guide, was not a whit better. As anarchy increased, immorality was likely to increase likewise; and Scotland was in danger of falling into such a state as that into which Poland fell, to its ruin, within a hundred and fifty years after; in which the savagery of feudalism, without its order or its chivalry, would be varnished over by a thin coating of French "civilization," and, as in the case of Bothwell, the vices of the court of Paris should be added to those of the Northern freebooter. To deliver Scotland from that ruin, it was needed that she should be united into one people, strong, not in mere political, but moral ideas; strong by the clear sense of right and wrong, by the belief in the government and the judgments of a living God. And the tone that Buchanan, like Knox, adopted concerning the great crimes of their day, helped notably that national salvation. It gathered together, organized, and strengthened, the scattered and wavering elements of public morality. It assured the hearts of all men who loved the right and hated the wrong; and taught a whole nation to call acts by their just names, whoever might be the doers of them. It appealed to the common conscience of men. It proclaimed a universal and God-given morality, a bar at which all, from the lowest to the highest, must alike be judged.

The tone was stern: but there was a need for sternness. Moral life and death were in the balance. If the Scots people were to be told that the crimes which roused their indignation were excusable, or beyond punishment, or to be hushed up and slipped over in any way, there was an end of morality among them. Every man, from the greatest to the least, would go and do likewise, according to his powers of evil. That method was being tried in France, and Spain likewise, during those very years. Notorious crimes were hushed up under the pretense of loyalty; excused as political necessities; smiled away as natural and pardonable weaknesses. The result was utter demodemoralizationth of France and Spain. Knox and Buchanan, the one from the standpoint of an old Hebrew prophet, the other rather from that of a Juvenal or a Tacitus, tried the other method, and called acts by their just names, appealing alike to conscience and to G The result was virtue and piety, and that manly independence of soul which is thought compatible with hearty loyalty, in a country labolaboringer heavy disadvantages, long divided almost into two hostile camps, two rival races.

And the good influence was soon manifest, not only in those who sided with Buchanan and his friends but in those who most opposed them. The Roman Catholic preachers, who at first asserted Mary's right to impurity while they allowed her guilt, grew silent for shame, and set themselves to assert her entire innocence; while the Scots who have followed their example have, to their honohonorken up the same ground. They have fought Buchanan on the ground of fact, not on the ground of morality: they have alleged--as they had a fair right to do--the probability of intrigue and forgery in an also profligate: the improbability that a Queen so gifted by nature and by fortune, and confessedly for a long while so strong and so spotless, should as it were by a suen insanity have proved so untrue to herself. Their noblest and purest sympathies have been enlisted--and who can blame them?--in loyalty to a Queen, chivalry to a woman, pity for the unfortunate and--as they conceived--the innocent; but whether they have been right or wrong in their view of facts, the Scotch partisans of Mary have always--as far as I know--been right in their view of morals; they have never deigned to admit Mary's guilt, and then to palliate it by those sentimental, or rather sensual, theories of human nature, too common in a certain school of French literature, too common, alas! in a certain school of modern English novels. They have not said, "She did it; but after all, was the deed so very inexcusable?" They have said, "The deed was inexcusable: but she did not do it." And so the Scotch admirers of Mary, who have numbered among them many a pure and noble, as well as many a gifted spirit, have kept at least themselves unstained; and have shown, whether consciously or not, that they too share in that sturdy Scotch moral sense which has been so much strengthened--as I believe by the plain speech of good old George Buchanan.

www.ingramcontent.com/pod-product-compliance
Lightning Source LLC
Chambersburg PA
CBHW061411160726

47995CB00002B/558